MARRIAGE BY DESIGN

MARRIAGE BY DESIGN

A Christian Couple's Guide to Building a Strong, God-centered Relationship

CARMEN WILDE

QuantumQuill Press

CONTENTS

Introduction

In the core of each and every marriage lies a potential that stretches out a long ways past the simple association of two people. It's a significant excursion that, when explored with aim and directed by divine standards, can prosper into a confirmation of adoration, beauty, and solidarity that reflects the actual heart of God. This book, "Marriage by Plan: A Christian Couple's Manual for Building Major areas of strength for a, focused Relationship," is created as a signal for the people who look for to travel through marriage as well as to flourish inside it, grounded in confidence and raised by divine love.

Our motivation is twofold. Right off the bat, we plan to enlighten the way that prompts a vigorous, God-focused marriage. A way frequently winds through landscapes of happiness, challenge, development, and in some cases, the valleys of gloom. However, with God as the foundation, each step is deliberate, each challenge conquerable, and each delight amplified. Through the insight of sacred text, the impressions of those who've strolled this way previously, and down to earth, significant direction, we look to outfit you with the devices essential for building and sustaining a relationship that perseveres as well as twists.

Besides, this book fills in as an encouragement to dive further into the profound elements of your association. Marriage, as planned by God, is in excess of an agreement; a contract repeats the resolute love and responsibility He has for us. It's a valuable chance to mirror His affection by they way we love one another, to develop together in friendship, however in character and in soul. By mooring your relationship in confidence, you make the way for a more significant, really satisfying, and endlessly more impressive type of adoration — one that rises above human blemish and mirrors the heavenly.

Whether you're setting out on the excursion of marriage, trying to develop a current relationship, or hoping to conquer difficulties through confidence, this book is for you. It's a guide, a buddy, and a wellspring of light for the excursion ahead, drawing from the everlasting great of integrity to direct you toward an adoration that endures as well as changes.

As we adventure through every part, let us approach with open hearts and psyches, prepared to investigate, comprehend, and apply the heavenly rules that can brace and enhance our conjugal bonds. Together, we should set out on this holy excursion, building a marriage that endures forever, however one that leaves a tradition of affection, confidence, and responsibility for a long time into the future.

The Significance of a Divine being focused Relationship

At the center of each and every getting through marriage is an establishment laid not on the moving sands of human inclination or the vaporous mainstays of common achievement, yet on the strong stone of confidence in God. The significance of a Divine being focused relationship couldn't possibly be more significant, for it is the actual heartbeat of a marriage that looks for to endure the unavoidable tempests as well as to flourish in the midst of them. This book support the rule that when God is set at the focal point of a marriage, He goes about as the compass that aides, the anchor that holds, and the fire that revives love, even in the coldest of winters.

A Divine being focused marriage offers a novel focal point through which couples can see their relationship, one that rises above the present time and place to embrace an everlasting viewpoint. It trains us to cherish with our feelings, however with an unshakable responsibility that repeats the relentlessness of God's affection for us. Such a viewpoint encourages persistence, sustains pardoning, and develops a dirt rich for development in the two accomplices. At the point when God's affection turns into the model for how we love one another, each thoughtful gesture, each token of friendship, and each word verbally expressed in affection turns into an impression of His effortlessness.

Besides, revolving your marriage around God imparts a feeling of direction that heads past private satisfaction or satisfaction. It changes the conjugal excursion into a heavenly mission, where the two accomplices are called to serve each other, support each other's profound development, and epitomize God's adoration to their general surroundings. This common mission reinforces the connection between companions, giving a shared objective that joins them in their excursion through life.

In the pages that follow, we will investigate the pragmatic manners by which couples can develop a Divine being focused relationship. From the everyday act of supplication and dedication, to the manners by which we impart, excuse, and backing each other, the accentuation will continuously be on how these activities mirror our adoration for God and, thusly, reinforce our affection for one another. By welcoming God into each part of your marriage, you hold nothing back from an extraordinary love that can endure the everyday hardships, preliminary, and change.

A Divine being focused marriage isn't just an ideal to yearn for; it is a no nonsense reality that is feasible for each couple able to put God first. As we dig further into the meaning of making God the foundation of your relationship, let us be enlivened by the commitment that what God has consolidated, no individual can isolate. In this heavenly organization, we track down the way in to an enduring marriage as well as the way to a more profound, really satisfying association with God Himself.

Construction of the Book

As we leave on this excursion together through "Marriage by Plan: A Christian Couple's Manual for Building Serious areas of strength for a, focused Relationship," it is gainful to comprehend the guide that will direct us through the investigation of building and sustaining a marriage that perseveres as well as flourishes under the direction of God's timeless insight. This book is organized to walk you, bit by bit, through the different features of a Christian marriage, offering both the other-worldly and reasonable direction vital for encouraging a relationship that lauds God at its center.

1. Underpinnings of a Faithful Marriage: Our process starts with laying out the bedrock of a Divine being focused marriage. Figuring out God's plan for marriage, the job of confidence, the force of petition, and the significance of responsibility makes way for the parts that follow. This essential information is vital for building a marriage that mirrors God's affection and reason.

2. Correspondence in Marriage: The craft of correspondence fills in as the backbone of a solid conjugal relationship. This part dives into the standards of Faithful correspondence, the meaning of undivided attention, and the beauty filled way to deal with settling clashes, all while accentuating the groundbreaking force of imploring together.

3. The Job of Pardoning and Elegance: Pushing ahead, we investigate the basic components of absolution and beauty in a marriage. Through scriptural bits of knowledge and pragmatic guidance, this part expects to furnish couples with the devices expected to explore the difficulties of pardoning, stretch out elegance to each other, and cultivate a culture of compromise and mending in their relationship.

4. Becoming Together In a profound way: The otherworldly excursion a couple embraces together is both individual and shared. This piece of the book centers around developing shared profound objectives, the significance of love and commitment as a team, the idea of otherworldly responsibility, and the delight of serving together, all of which add to a more profound, more significant association with God and one another.

5. Sustaining Closeness in Marriage: Closeness, in its many structures, is the string that winds around the texture of a solid marriage. This part tends to the components of closeness — profound, otherworldly, and physical — and offers direction on keeping a dynamic association, conquering deterrents to closeness, and the job of petitioning God in extending the personal connection between mates.

6. Monetary Stewardship in a Christian Marriage: Perceiving the frequently complicated job of funds in a marriage, this segment gives scriptural standards of stewardship, pragmatic counsel on planning together, the significance of liberality, and entrusting God with your funds, all pointed toward cultivating solidarity and confidence in this crucial area of conjugal life.

7. Nurturing and Day to day Life: For couples favored with the obligation of nurturing, this section tends to bringing up youngsters inside the structure of confidence, adjusting the conjugal and parental jobs, and overseeing associations with more distant family, all while keeping the conjugal relationship as the primary need.

8. Conquering Difficulties Together: No marriage is without its preliminaries, however every test presents a chance for development and extending of the conjugal bond. This last section offers systems for recognizing and dealing with difficulties directly, the job of local area and church support, recharging responsibility in difficult stretches, and motivating declarations of couples who have endured storms through confidence and responsibility.

End: Proceeding with the Excursion Together: As we close this aide, an intelligent outline underscores the continuous idea of development in marriage, the significance of keeping God at the middle, and a devout farewell for the excursion ahead, loaded up with trust, love, and heavenly direction.

Every part is planned not exclusively to give knowledge and exhortation yet additionally to empower profound, significant conversations among companions and inside the more extensive Christian people group. By following this organized way, couples are welcome to leave on an extraordinary excursion towards a marriage that endures the everyday hardships as well as twists in the finesse of God's affection and direction.

Chapter 1: Foundations of a Godly Marriage

Figuring out God's Plan for Marriage

Before all else, God made marriage as a hallowed contract, a heavenly embroidery woven with strings of affection, organization, and reason. To comprehend the underpinnings of a Faithful marriage, we should initially turn our hearts and psyches to the Maker's unique plan, as framed in the Sacred texts. This heavenly outline offers us not just a brief look into the core of God yet additionally a guide for building our conjugal connections in arrangement with His will.

God's plan for marriage is established in friendship, solidarity, and shared help. All along, in the Nursery of Eden, obviously people were made for relationship — with God as well as with each other. "It isn't really great for the man to be distant from everyone else," God pronounced, featuring the inborn requirement for friendship and association that is woven into the actual texture of our being (Beginning 2:18). In light of this need, God made an accomplice, a partner reasonable for man, laying out the principal marriage as a model of friendship and shared help.

This organization was intended to be God's very own impression character — His affection, His dedication, and His obligation to His kin. Marriage, in this manner, isn't just a human establishment yet a heavenly one, expected to reflect the solidarity and love tracked down inside the actual Trinity. A contract goes past the physical and profound association of two individuals; an otherworldly bond mirrors the pledge connection among Christ and His Congregation (Ephesians 5:25-32). In this heavenly association, married couples are called to cherish each other magnanimously, conciliatorily, and genuinely, similarly as Christ adores the Congregation.

Moreover, God's plan for marriage envelops the idea of "one tissue" (Beginning 2:24). This significant secret discusses a solidarity that rises above the physical, typifying profound, otherworldly, and scholarly unity. An all encompassing association cultivates closeness, development, and shared enlightenment. In becoming one tissue, life partners leave on an excursion of turning out to be more similar to Christ, permitting their union with be a demonstration of God's blessing work in their lives.

Understanding God's plan for marriage makes way for a relationship based on the strong underpinning of heavenly truth. It welcomes couples to see their marriage as an individual satisfaction try as well as a heavenly calling to mirror God's affection to one another and their general surroundings. As we adjust our union with God's plan, we open ourselves to the completion of His gifts, encountering the genuine profundity, delight, and motivation behind being joined in blessed marriage.

The Job of Confidence in Marriage

Inside the hallowed contract of marriage, confidence goes about as both the anchor and the compass, directing couples through the rhythmic movement of life's seasons. The job of confidence in marriage is diverse, stretching out a long ways past individual convictions to shape the actual embodiment of the conjugal relationship. Through confidence couples track down the solidarity to explore difficulties, the effortlessness to pardon, and the desire to push forward, in any event, when the way forward appears to be darkened.

Confidence in God acquaints a significant aspect with marriage, changing it from a simple human understanding into a heavenly responsibility. From this perspective of confidence couples can see their marriage as a living declaration of God's dedication and love. This viewpoint urges life partners to depend not on their own comprehension or strength but rather on the insight and force of God. Axioms 3:5-6 reminds us to "Entrust in the Ruler with your entire being and lean not on your own comprehension; in the entirety of your ways submit to him, and he will make your ways straight." In marriage, this trust includes resting on God for direction, strength, and shrewdness in each part of the relationship, from correspondence and compromise to closeness and nurturing.

Besides, confidence fills in as a bringing together power, bringing couples nearer not exclusively to one another yet additionally to God. It cultivates a common profound excursion, where companions can fill together in their affection for God and for each other. This common excursion is set apart by shared consolation, where each accomplice upholds the other's profound development, provokes them to experience their confidence in viable ways, and stands adjacent to them in the midst of profound dry spell or uncertainty.

The job of confidence in marriage likewise envelops the act of otherworldly disciplines inside the relationship. Petition, love, and the investigation of Sacred writing become individual propensities as well as aggregate demonstrations of dedication that reinforce the conjugal bond. Such practices empower couples to look for God's will together, to figure out something worth agreeing on in shared values and convictions, and to encounter the profound delight of being joined in reason and soul.

At last, confidence in marriage goes about as the establishment whereupon a Divine being focused relationship is constructed. It welcomes God into the relationship, not as a far off onlooker, but rather as a functioning member, guide, and ally. By setting confidence at the focal point of their marriage, couples can explore the intricacies of existence with certainty, realizing that they are maintained by God's constant love and dependability. In this heavenly organization, marriage turns into an excursion of shared development, significant satisfaction, and getting through adoration, secured solidly in the loyalty of God.

Petition: The Foundation of Solidarity

In the hallowed engineering of a Faithful marriage, petitioning God fills in as the foundation of solidarity, restricting the hearts of life partners along with the core of God. Through petitioning God couples welcome the Heavenly into their regular routines, looking for His direction, intelligence, and gift over their association. This demonstration of shared weakness and otherworldly closeness encourages a significant connection between accomplices, making a groundwork of trust, understanding, and common help that can face the hardships of life.

Petition in marriage isn't just a custom or a rundown of solicitations introduced to God; it is a discourse — a no nonsense discussion that welcomes God to talk into the relationship. At these times of calm acquiescence couples can reveal their hearts, their feelings of dread, their expectations, and their fantasies, not exclusively to one another however to their Maker. This common profound practice turns into a wellspring of solidarity and harmony, from which couples can draw when confronted with difficulties, choices, or the unremarkable minutes that contain the texture of hitched life.

Also, petitioning heaven has the novel ability to change the common into the holy, to raise the preliminaries and wins of marriage into open doors for otherworldly development and more profound association. At the point when couples supplicate together, they recognize their reliance on God, perceiving that He supports their affection, braces their responsibility, and guides their excursion. This demonstration of aggregate confidence fills in as a strong update that they are in good company in their excursion, that their marriage is under the careful focus and cherishing care of God.

The foundation of petitioning God likewise assumes a urgent part in encouraging pardoning and compromise inside the marriage. As couples look for God's effortlessness together, they are helped to remember His boundless pardoning towards them, motivating them to stretch out a similar elegance to one another. In the modest demonstration of petitioning God for and with each other, hindrances of pride and disdain can be destroyed, making ready for recuperating, understanding, and a restored obligation to cherish as Christ loves.

Petition, hence, isn't simply an establishment for correspondence with God yet a crucial life saver that interfaces the hearts of mates to one another and to their Maker. Through this heavenly exchange couples can find the genuine embodiment of solidarity — a solidarity not based on transient feelings or common guidelines, but rather on the unshakeable commitments of God. As couples focus on making supplication the foundation of their marriage, they construct their relationship upon an establishment that can't be shaken, moored in the timeless love and dependability of God.

Chapter 2: Communication in Marriage

The Craft of Authentic Correspondence

In the embroidery of marriage, the strings of correspondence wind around together the texture of association, understanding, and closeness. Genuine correspondence, mixed with the standards of adoration, regard, and trustworthiness, fills in as the establishment for a flourishing, God-focused marriage. Through this heavenly workmanship couples can genuinely tune in, comprehend, and associate with each other on a profoundly otherworldly and close to home level.

The embodiment of Genuine correspondence lies in the obligation to talk and tune in affection. Ephesians 4:15 urges us to "talk reality in affection," an order that highlights the harmony among genuineness and sympathy. With regards to marriage, this implies offering viewpoints, sentiments, and needs transparently and truly, however consistently with a heart of adoration and a longing for the prosperity of the other. It is tied in with picking words that development as opposed to destroy, that support instead of deter.

Moreover, Faithful correspondence includes undivided attention — an expertise that requires hearing words, however looking to figure out the heart behind them. James 1:19 reminds us to "rush to tune in, slow to talk and ease back to end up being furious." This sacred text features the significance of tuning in as a demonstration of adoration and regard. At the point when couples listen effectively, they approve each other's sentiments and viewpoints, making a place of refuge for weakness and trust to thrive.

Rehearsing Faithful correspondence likewise implies being aware of what is said, yet the way things are said. The manner of speaking, non-verbal communication, and, surprisingly, the planning of a discussion can essentially influence how messages are gotten. Precepts 15:1 instructs that "a delicate response dismisses fury, yet a cruel word works up outrage." This intelligence urges couples to move toward every discussion with tenderness and responsiveness, perceiving the force of their words to either mend or damage.

At its center, Faithful correspondence is God's very own impression correspondence with us — loaded up with beauty, tolerance, and love. It is a device that God gives couples to construct closeness, resolve clashes, and fill together in their excursion towards a more significant comprehension of one another and of God's motivation for their marriage.

As we dive further into the specialty of Faithful correspondence, let us recollect that it isn't only an expertise to be dominated, yet a sacrosanct practice to be lived out everyday. Through this heavenly specialty of correspondence couples can reinforce their bond, extend their association, and fabricate a marriage that praises God in each word verbally expressed and heard.

Tuning in as a Demonstration of Affection

In the ensemble of marriage, where words are the notes and understanding the song, listening arises not simply as a latent demonstration, but rather as a significant articulation of adoration. To tune in — to genuinely tune in — is to offer one's heart, consideration, and presence to their accomplice, asserting their worth and the profundity of the relationship. This section investigates the groundbreaking force of tuning in as a demonstration of adoration, a fundamental part of Faithful correspondence that supports trust, encourages closeness, and works with the development of a solid, God-focused marriage.

Undivided attention in marriage rises above the simple hear-able handling of words verbally expressed by one's companion. It includes drawing in with sympathy, trying to grasp the substance as well as the feelings, aims, and wants fundamental the words. This type of listening mirrors the manner in which God pays attention to us — with persistence, sympathy, and a steady spotlight on our souls. Similarly as Hymn 116:1-2 uncovers, "I love the Ruler, for he heard my voice; he heard my sob for leniency. Since he turned his ear to me, I will approach him as long as I live." Comparatively, when companions turn their ears to one another with similar mindfulness and care, they epitomize God's adoration in their marriage.

Tuning in as a demonstration of adoration requires the saving of one's own considerations, decisions, and interruptions to completely go into the experience of the other. It implies hushing the inward voice that rushes to figure out reactions or guards, and on second thought, opening the heart to hear and sympathize with the other's point of view genuinely. This benevolent demonstration of really focusing is a strong certification of the other's worth and a demonstration of the prioritization of the relationship over individual inner selves or plans.

Moreover, compelling listening cultivates a climate where weakness is invited and treasured. It guarantees accomplices that they are seen, heard, and esteemed, establishing a groundwork for more profound close to home and otherworldly closeness. In the security of this climate, couples can all the more unreservedly express their expectations, fears, and dreams, positive about the information that they are upheld and perceived.

The act of tuning in as a demonstration of affection likewise assumes a basic part in compromise inside marriage. By endeavoring to comprehend prior to being perceived, couples can explore conflicts with effortlessness and compassion, frequently uncovering basic issues and pursuing goal in a way that fortifies as opposed to debilitates their bond.

As we venture through the craft of tuning in, let us embrace it as an expertise to be grown, however as a gift to be proposed to our companion. In doing as such, we mirror the listening heart of God, cultivating a marriage where love isn't recently spoken, however showed through the significant demonstration of tuning in.

Exploring Struggle with Elegance

In the nursery of marriage, struggle is an unavoidable weed that, whenever maneuvered carefully, can be evacuated in a way that improves the dirt, making the relationship stronger and delightful. This part dives into the specialty of exploring struggle with elegance, a basic expertise for any couple looking to develop serious areas of strength for a, focused marriage. From the perspective of effortlessness couples can change potential hindrances into venturing stones towards more profound comprehension and solidarity.

Beauty in struggle implies moving toward conflicts with a heart of empathy, modesty, and persistence, perceiving that the two accomplices are unsteady people endeavoring to typify Christ's affection. It's a sign of Ephesians 4:2-3, which urges us to "Be totally unassuming and delicate; show restraint, holding on for each other in affection. Really bend over backward to keep the solidarity of the Soul through the obligation of harmony." Moving toward struggle with this outlook doesn't mean keeping away from conflicts however confronting them in a manner that mirrors God's adoration and encourages harmony.

To explore struggle with effortlessness, couples should initially look to see as opposed to be perceived. This includes effectively paying attention to one another's points of view without judgment, recognizing sentiments, and approving encounters. It's tied in with seeing the issue according to the next's perspective and taking a stab at compassion in any event, when feelings run high. Such a methodology can diffuse strain and make a place of refuge for open, legit exchange.

Also, elegance in struggle includes talking reality in affection. This implies offering one's viewpoints and sentiments genuinely however with benevolence and regard, staying away from cruel words that can wound and leave enduring scars. Precepts 15:1 instructs, "A delicate response dismisses rage, yet a cruel word works up outrage." By picking words that recuperate instead of harmed, couples can resolve issues productively, preparing for shared understanding and goal.

Besides, exploring struggle with elegance requires pardoning and an eagerness to relinquish feelings of hatred. Clutching complaints can harm the relationship, though pardoning liberates the two accomplices from the chains of past damages, permitting them to push ahead with a lighter heart. Colossians 3:13 supports, "Hold on for one another and pardon each other on the off chance that any of you has a complaint against somebody. Excuse as the Master pardoned you." This heavenly charge features absolution as a vital part of elegance filled compromise, fundamental for the wellbeing and development of the marriage.

Finally, exploring struggle with effortlessness implies focusing on goal and development. It's really not necessary to focus on winning a contention yet about fortifying the obligation of marriage. This responsibility includes looking for arrangements that consider the two accomplices' requirements and cooperating towards compromise and solidarity. An excursion might require split the difference, change, and, in particular, supplication, looking for God's insight and direction constantly.

As couples embrace the test of exploring struggle with effortlessness, they develop a marriage that mirrors the generous, understanding, and never-ending adoration for Christ. It's through these preliminaries that the foundations of their relationship develop further, attracting them nearer to one another and to God, sustained by the elegance that streams from His heart.

Chapter 3: The Role of Forgiveness and Grace

Grasping Pardoning in a Christian Marriage

In the holy contract of marriage, pardoning isn't simply a choice yet a central edict, repeating the core of God's effortlessness towards us. The excursion to understanding pardoning inside the setting of a Christian marriage starts by digging into the scriptural establishments that support this heavenly order. Sacred text is packed with lessons and models that highlight pardoning as a demonstration of adoration, an impression of God's personality, and a fundamental way to mending and reclamation.

Scriptural Groundworks of Pardoning

The quintessence of pardoning in marriage is established in the actual gospel. Ephesians 4:32 educates us to "be caring to each other, gracious, pardoning each other, as God in Christ excused you." This section not just orders pardoning as our very own impression excused status in Christ yet in addition sets it as the norm for all connections inside the Christian people group, including marriage. It fills in as a strong update that pardoning isn't dependent upon the seriousness of the offense yet on the greatness of the elegance we most definitely have gotten.

The Effect of Unforgiveness

Holding onto unforgiveness in the core of a marriage is similar to permitting a toxin to saturate the dirt of adoration, trust, and closeness that supports the relationship. Unforgiveness breeds harshness, outrage, and disdain — feelings that can dissolve the groundwork of a marriage, prompting profound distance and otherworldly detachment. It goes about as a boundary to correspondence, closeness, and development, getting couples into a pattern of agony and counter that can pulverize the conjugal bond.

Pardoning as a Choice and Interaction

Pardoning in marriage rises above the oversimplified thought of neglecting or pardoning bad behavior. It is a purposeful choice to let one's companion out of the obligation of their offense, a decision that reflects God's pardoning of our transgressions. In any case, it is similarly essential to perceive pardoning as a cycle — an excursion that includes managing the hurt, grasping the effect of the offense, and effectively deciding to relinquish disdain and sharpness.

This cycle demands investment, persistence, and, frequently, a co-ordinated work to reconstruct trust and closeness. It's not necessary to focus on denying the aggravation or imagining the offense never happened however about pursuing a cognizant choice to not allow it to characterize or obliterate the relationship. Through absolution, couples can view as mending and rebuilding, transforming wounds into scars that vouch for the strength and profundity of their affection and responsibility.

As we investigate the basic job of pardoning in a Christian marriage, it is crucial for approach it not as a difficult obligation but rather as a freeing demonstration of adoration that mirrors the actual heart of the Gospel. In doing as such, we make the way for more profound as-sociation, recharged closeness, and a more grounded, stronger conjugal bond, grounded in the beauty and love of Christ.

The Method involved with Excusing

Setting out on the excursion of pardoning inside the holy limits of marriage is to explore a way that is both significantly testing and profoundly recuperating. This cycle, fundamental for the wellbeing and essentialness of the relationship, requires a conscious and genuine methodology, supported by the effortlessness and love that streams from our relationship with Christ. Understanding and taking part in the moves toward absolution can change the unavoidable damages of hitched life into amazing open doors for development, more profound closeness, and getting through solidarity.

Moves toward Pardoning

The underlying move toward the pardoning system includes recognizing the aggravation. It's urgent for the hurt party to sincerely defy the feelings and hurt brought about by their life partner's activities or words, without limiting or excusing their sentiments. This straightforwardness is the establishment for authentic recuperating and compromise.

Following this affirmation, sympathy assumes an essential part. Endeavoring to see what is going on according to the viewpoint of the person who caused the hurt can be testing, yet it cultivates understanding and empathy. It's tied in with perceiving that we are error prone creatures needing beauty. This step doesn't pardon the way of behaving however permits us to see our life partner completely, not exclusively characterized by their misstep.

Choosing to pardon is the foundation of this excursion. A decision frequently conflicts with our normal tendencies toward reprisal or holding feelings of resentment. This choice is less about the sensations existing apart from everything else and more about a guarantee to the wellbeing and eventual fate of the marriage. It's a strong demonstration of will, upheld by supplication and a craving to comply with God's order to pardon as we have been excused.

Looking for Pardoning

For the one looking for pardoning, the cycle includes an earnest affirmation of bad behavior and a bona fide expression of remorse. This step isn't simply about saying "Please accept my apologies" yet about communicating a comprehension of the effect of one's activities and a veritable regret for the aggravation caused. It incorporates a guarantee to change conduct and offer to set things straight, exhibiting a genuine contrition that goes beyond anything that can be described.

Pardoning Yourself

A frequently disregarded yet similarly significant part of absolution is self-pardoning. The excursion towards pardoning oneself for causing torment in the marriage can be laden with responsibility and disgrace. In any case, embracing God's pardon for our wrongdoings and errors permits us to stretch out that equivalent effortlessness to ourselves. Self-pardoning isn't tied in with vindicating ourselves of obligation yet about tolerating God's beauty, gaining from our mix-ups, and pushing ahead with a pledge to improve.

The most common way of pardoning in a Christian marriage is a demonstration of the groundbreaking force of God's adoration and elegance. It's an excursion that mends and reestablishes as well as extends the profound and close to home connection between companions. By strolling this way, couples can arise more grounded, stronger, and all the more profoundly dedicated to mirroring Christ's adoration in each part of their marriage.

Compromise and Recuperating

The excursion through pardoning in the core of a marriage normally prompts the consecrated ground of compromise and mending. This last stage during the time spent absolution is where the genuine reclamation of the relationship starts to prosper, directed by the standards of elegance, love, and common responsibility. Here couples can reconstruct the scaffolds that were harmed or broken by destructive activities or words, creating a more grounded, stronger bond that is equipped for enduring the hardships of coexistence.

Building Scaffolds After Pardoning

The demonstration of pardoning lays the preparation for compromise, however it is the deliberate strides towards revamping trust and closeness that set the mending system. This starts with open, legitimate correspondence about the hurt that happened, the effect it had on each accomplice, and the apprehensions and expectations for the fate of the relationship. Such discussions, however possibly troublesome, are imperative for getting the trash free from past damages and false impressions, accounting for new development.

A urgent part of modifying trust is the reliable exhibit of changed conduct. Activities, in this unique situation, express stronger than words. The accomplice who made the hurt has the obligation show, through their activities and decisions, their obligation to the prosperity of the relationship and their mate. This could include defining clear limits, looking for responsibility, or going with unmistakable changes in conduct or choice making processes.

The Job of Petitioning heaven in Mending

Petitioning heaven assumes a basic part in the compromise and mending process. It is through petition that the two accomplices can look for the insight, strength, and direction of God as they explore the intricate feelings and difficulties of revamping their relationship. Petitioning heaven likewise fills in for of giving the agony and the cycle over to God, confiding in His timing and plan for the total reclamation of the conjugal bond. Couples can track down solace, trust, and mending in the affirmation of God's presence and dynamic work in their relationship.

Keeping a Generous and Charitable Heart

The excursion towards a completely mended and accommodated marriage is progressing and requires a nonstop obligation to keeping a generous and benevolent heart. This includes a day to day decision to relinquish harshness, to expand effortlessness despite blemishes, and to pick love in any event, when it is troublesome. It likewise implies embracing a stance of lowliness, perceiving that the two accomplices are needing effortlessness and pardoning, from one another as well as from God.

Couples are urged to develop a culture of pardoning and effortlessness inside their marriage, perceiving these temperances as fundamental elements for a sound, flourishing relationship. Thusly, they shield their marriage against future damages as well as make a space where love, trust, and closeness can develop and thrive.

In embracing the standards of compromise and recuperating, couples vouch for the redemptive force of God's affection and beauty in their marriage. That's what they exhibit, through pardoning and a pledge to reconstructing their relationship, it is feasible to rise out of the flames of harmed and struggle with a bond that is more grounded, further, and stronger than any time in recent memory.

Chapter 4: Growing Together Spiritually

Developing Shared Otherworldly Objectives

In the excursion of marriage, becoming together in a deep sense isn't simply a desire yet a central component that can hoist the association to mirror the profundity and magnificence of God's plan for this hallowed contract. Fundamental to this profound development is the development of shared otherworldly objectives, a cycle that requires deliberateness, common comprehension, and a promise to stroll in confidence together.

Setting Profound Targets Together

The most important phase in this excursion is for couples to meet up in pious reflection to distinguish their otherworldly targets. This includes transparent conversations about every individual's otherworldly longings, the regions they feel God is calling them to fill in, and how these goals unite inside the setting of their marriage. Whether it's developing comprehension they might interpret the Sacred writings, filling in supplication, or encapsulating Christ's affection in their cooperations with others, laying out these objectives as a team makes a brought together vision for their otherworldly excursion.

This cycle additionally permits couples to perceive and commend their novel profound gifts and how these can be blended to serve God and each other in their marriage. It's tied in with recognizing that while they are two people, they are called to fill one brought together need under God's heavenly arrangement.

Coordinating Confidence into Day to day existence

With shared profound objectives set, the subsequent stage is incorporating these goals into the texture of day to day existence. This combination reinvigorates the couple's otherworldly goals, changing them from conceptual ideas into living articulations of their confidence. It could include carving out opportunity every day for joint petition and Sacred writing perusing, devoting minutes to talk about profound matters, or simply deciding — of all shapes and sizes — with their common confidence as the core value.

Useful combination of confidence into day to day existence additionally implies perceiving and quickly taking advantage of the workable opportunities that God presents, permitting the Essence of God to direct discussions, choices, and even contentions. It includes making a family culture where profound objectives are examined as well as lived out, impacting each part of the couple's coexistence from how they oversee funds, to how they bring up kids, to how they collaborate with their more extensive local area.

The development of shared otherworldly objectives is much the same as sowing seeds in a nursery that the two accomplices delicately care for. It requires customary supporting, persistence, and the readiness to adjust and become together. As these objectives flourish and start to thrive, they improve the couple's profound life as well as reinforce their bond, making a marriage that genuinely mirrors the greatness and beauty of God. This real excursion of shared otherworldly development, supported by common objectives and everyday mix, turns into a reference point of light — for the couple as well as for all who witness their association.

The Significance of Love and Dedication as a Team

In the consecrated excursion of marriage, love and dedication are not simply individual demonstrations of trust but rather shared encounters that tight spot the hearts of couples nearer to one another and to God.

The development of a daily schedule for shared love and dedication is similar to watering the seeds of profound objectives planted together, guaranteeing they develop profound roots and prove to be fruitful that supports both the relationship and their general surroundings.

Making a Daily practice for Shared Love

The underpinning of areas of strength for a, energetic marriage is much of the time found in the calm minutes spent within the sight of God, one next to the other. Laying out an everyday practice for shared love and commitment includes saving committed time for these profound works on, focusing on them in the midst of the hecticness of day to day existence. This could mean starting every day with supplication, devoting nights to concentrate on Sacred writing together, or participating in love at a nearby gathering or inside the home. The mood of customary, shared commitment shapes an otherworldly help for the marriage, a hallowed space where couples can interface with the heavenly and with each other on a significant level.

This routine ought to be adaptable, regarding the regular recurring pattern of life's requests, yet it should likewise be deliberate, watching this time against the bunch interruptions that can cheapen otherworldly development. It's tied in with finding what works for the couple, whether it's investigating a Book of scriptures concentrate on plan together, taking part in a request challenge, or essentially sitting peacefully before God. The key is consistency and the shared obligation to sustain their profound association.

Extending Otherworldly Closeness Through Love

Taking part in love and commitment together accomplishes something beyond satisfy a profound obligation; it makes the way for more profound closeness. As couples share their considerations, reflections, and disclosures gathered from their reflection time, they welcome each other into their profound excursion, sharing weaknesses and seeing each other's development in confidence. This weakness is the bedrock of closeness, making a bond that isn't handily shaken by life's preliminaries.

Besides, shared love and dedication give a special focal point through which couples can see their relationship and their general surroundings. It adjusts their hearts and psyches to God's motivations, directing them in navigation, compromise, and the day to day articulation of affection and beauty. Through love, they are helped to remember God's power and love, encouraging a feeling of appreciation and stunningness that pervades their relationship.

The effect of customary, shared love on a marriage couldn't possibly be more significant. At these times of aggregate dedication couples track down strength, direction, and solace. They figure out how to incline not on their own seeing but rather on the commitments of God, moving nearer to Him and, thusly, to one another. As they lift their voices in petition and recognition, they weave a more grounded, stronger texture of affection and responsibility, creating a marriage that stands as a demonstration of the force of confidence lived out together.

Profound Responsibility and Backing

In the hallowed undertaking of building a marriage that mirrors the core of God, the standards of otherworldly responsibility and backing stand as support points, reinforcing the underpinning of the relationship. This component of conjugal development is where the confidence venture becomes a special goal as well as a shared responsibility, where life partners empower and maintain each other in their stroll with Christ. It is inside this setting that the genuine profundity of profound friendship is understood, cultivating a marriage that blossoms with common support, trustworthiness, and a common quest for righteousness.

Jobs of Responsibility Accomplices in Marriage

Otherworldly responsibility in marriage rises above the customary standards of responsibility; it is established in affection, trust, and a profound longing for the profound prosperity of one's companion. As responsibility accomplices, couples set out on an excursion where they can straightforwardly share their battles, triumphs, questions, and experiences, realizing they will be met with understanding and effortlessness. This job includes tenderly testing each other to experience their confidence legitimately and gallantly, whether it's through keeping up with predictable reflection propensities, living out scriptural standards in day to day existence, or serving their local area and church.

The embodiment of being responsibility accomplices is tracked down in the sensitive harmony among support and remedy. It's tied in with being a mirror for one's mate, reflecting back to them not just their inborn worth and likely in Christ yet additionally regions where development is required. This requires a feeling of lowliness and tenderness, suggestive of Galatians 6:1, which trains, "Family, assuming that somebody is trapped in a transgression, you who live by the Soul ought to reestablish that individual delicately. Yet, watch yourselves, or you additionally might be enticed."

Building a Strong Otherworldly People group

While the responsibility between mates is vital, the more extensive Christian people group assumes an irreplaceable part in supporting and enhancing the couple's otherworldly excursion. This people group — whether tracked down in a nearby church, little gathering, or circle of Christian companions — gives a drawn out organization of shrewdness, consolation, and pragmatic help. Drawing in with a local area of devotees offers different points of view and encounters, improving the couple's comprehension and practice of confidence. It likewise gives a security net, offering direction, petition, and help with critical crossroads or emergency.

Building a strong otherworldly local area includes deliberate commitment with friends in faith, partaking in collective love, Book of scriptures studies, and partnership exercises. About making and sustaining connections are based on a shared love for Christ and a longing to fill in confidence. For wedded couples, this local area turns into an important asset, offering models of faithful relationships, mentorship valuable open doors, and the aggregate insight of the people who have explored comparable difficulties and delights.

The interweaving of otherworldly responsibility and backing inside marriage and the more extensive Christian people group makes a vigorous structure for profound development. It guarantees that couples are not strolling their confidence process in seclusion but rather are encircled by a haze of witnesses who cheer them on, support them, and help them to remember the beauty and truth tracked down in Jesus Christ. In this sacrosanct organization, the excursion of confidence turns into a common experience, set apart by development, flexibility, and an extending love for God and one another.

Serving Together in Confidence

The demonstration of serving together structures a vital strand in the entwining of lives inside a Christian marriage, restricting couples nearer to one another and to God. It is through help that confidence becomes dynamic, love becomes unmistakable, and the otherworldly excursion divided among life partners takes on a significant collective aspect. This common help isn't just about the actual demonstrations however about exemplifying the adoration and modesty of Christ, making the marriage a living declaration to His elegance and sympathy.

Recognizing Open doors for Joint Help

The excursion towards serving together starts with the ID of chances that resound with the two accomplices, lining up with their common interests, otherworldly gifts, and the requirements of their local area. This could go from chipping in at neighborhood covers, taking part in chapel services, or taking part in mission work, to more modest thoughtful gestures inside their nearby circles. The key is finding roads where their consolidated endeavors can mirror the adoration for Christ to other people, having an effect in substantial, significant ways.

This cycle includes pious thought and open conversation, looking for God's direction to reveal where their joint assistance can be best. About perceiving several has an extraordinary mix of gifts and assets that God plans for them to use in support of others. At the point when couples serve together, they enhance their effect as well as extend how they might interpret one another and of God's motivation for their marriage.

The Effect of Administration on Marriage

Serving together groundbreakingly affects a marriage, improving it in manners that go past the quick advantages of the help performed. It cultivates a feeling of solidarity and reason, as couples experience the delight and satisfaction that come from sacrificially giving of themselves. This common experience of serving others can likewise give a new viewpoint on their own endowments and difficulties, developing a more profound feeling of appreciation and satisfaction inside their relationship.

Besides, confronting the difficulties and awards of administration together fortifies the conjugal bond. It requires collaboration, correspondence, and common help, characteristics that are fundamental for a solid marriage. As couples explore the intricacies of serving others, they figure out how to depend on one another's assets, pardon each other's shortcomings, and commend their achievements together. This common excursion of administration turns into a strong impetus for development, both exclusively and as a couple.

The demonstration of serving together likewise fills in as a strong observer to the adoration for Christ. It exemplifies the scriptural standard of adoration in real life, showing the world a brief look at God's realm through the solidarity and liberality of a Divine being focused marriage. As couples spill out adoration and administration to other people, they mirror the conciliatory love of Christ, drawing others towards Him and advancing their own relationship simultaneously.

All in all, serving together in confidence isn't just a movement for Christian couples however a fundamental part of their otherworldly excursion together. It is through assistance that confidence is lived without holding back, affection is given hands and feet, and relationships are based on the strong stone of Christ's model. As couples focus on serving together, they weave a more grounded, more dynamic embroidery of affection, for one another as well as for their general surroundings.

Chapter 5: Nurturing Intimacy in Marriage

Investigating the Elements of Closeness

Closeness, the actual heartbeat of a conjugal relationship, is a multi-layered pearl that mirrors the profundity, excellence, and intricacy of two spirits woven together in a pledge of affection. To support closeness is to watch out for the nursery of marriage with perseverance and care, guaranteeing that each aspect — profound, otherworldly, and physical — gets the consideration and sustenance it necessities to prosper.

Profound Closeness: The foundation of a profound and persevering through association between mates lies in the domain of close to home closeness. This aspect is based on an underpinning of trust, receptiveness, and weakness, where hearts are uncovered and the most profound apprehensions, dreams, and sentiments are shared without reservation. Developing profound closeness requires undivided attention, sympathy, and a resolute obligation to grasping one's accomplice past the surface level. It's tied in with making a place of refuge where every individual feels esteemed, heard, and profoundly associated with the other.

Otherworldly Closeness: At the spirit of a Divine being focused marriage is otherworldly closeness, a significant bond that develops from shared confidence, values, and commitment. This sacrosanct association is sustained through joint petition, love, and the quest for God's motivation for the relationship. Otherworldly closeness welcomes God into each part of the marriage, looking for His direction, observing His presence, and serving Him together. In this common otherworldly excursion couples track down strength, heading, and a more profound feeling of solidarity, secured in their aggregate love for and confidence in God.

Actual Closeness: The declaration of affection through actual touch and closeness is one more fundamental part of closeness in marriage. Actual closeness incorporates something beyond sexual connection; it incorporates the delicate contacts, warm hugs, and delicate demonstrations of fondness that convey love and care. Inside the obligations of marriage, actual closeness is a delightful festival of affection, intended to fortify the conjugal association and support the eliteness and profundity of the relationship. It requires continuous correspondence, common regard, and a promise to satisfying each other's necessities and wants in a cherishing and caring way.

Sustaining closeness in marriage implies concentrating on every one of these aspects, it are profoundly interconnected and similarly essential to perceive that they. It's tied in with pursuing everyday decisions to associate, share, and be available with each other, purposely winding around together the strings of profound, profound, and actual closeness. By embracing the full range of closeness, couples can fabricate a marriage that gets by as well as flourishes, mirroring the magnificence and profundity of God's plan for this sacrosanct association.

Keeping Affection Alive

In the excursion of marriage, the flares of adoration are not self-maintaining; they require steady sustaining, deliberate attention, and the fuel of genuine activities to stay energetic and warm. Keeping love alive is a craftsmanship and a responsibility, a progression of day to day decisions that revive the core of the relationship, guaranteeing that it develops further and more gorgeous as time passes.

Normal Articulations of Adoration: Love, in its most veritable structure, isn't recently felt yet effectively communicated. The everyday insistences of adoration — be it through encouraging statements, demonstrations of administration, smart gifts, quality time, or actual touch — act as the soul of the conjugal relationship. These articulations are the language of adoration spoken between two hearts, conveying worth, appreciation, and profound fondness. Couples ought to endeavor to comprehend and communicate in their mate's way to express affection fluidly, guaranteeing that their tokens of adoration are both significant and gotten with the glow with which they are expected.

Date Evenings and Quality Time: In the midst of the rushing about of day to day existence, cutting out time for date evenings and quality minutes together is fundamental for keeping love alive. These devoted times, liberated from the interruptions and requests of the rest of the world, offer couples an open door to reconnect, rediscover, and develop their closeness. Whether it's a basic home-prepared dinner partook in candlelight, a stroll under the stars, or an arranged trip to a position of shared revenue, these minutes are loved chances to support the relationship and reaffirm the need of the conjugal bond.

Dealing with Life's Difficulties Together: The way of marriage is one that will definitely cross through times of satisfaction and times of challenge. Keeping love alive means confronting these seasons connected at the hip, supporting each other through the preliminaries and gathering together to celebrate in the victories. It includes a promise to cooperation, utilizing the strength of the organization to explore life's difficulties. This common excursion through the ups and downs tests the versatility of the relationship as well as fortifies the power of profound devotion, manufacturing a more profound solidarity and shared regard.

Keeping love alive in marriage is a conscious excursion of constant pursuit, a dance of extending closeness and warmth that develops and develops after some time. It requires innovativeness, industriousness, and in particular, a heart that is completely dedicated to treasuring and developing the adoration divided among two spirits. As couples put resources into this holy undertaking, they make a tradition of affection that enhances their own lives as well as moves people around them, mirroring the getting through excellence of an affection that genuinely endures forever.

Beating Snags to Closeness

In the sacrosanct excursion of marriage, the way to keeping up with and developing closeness is frequently flung with deterrents. These difficulties, whether they come from inside the relationship or from outside pressures, can create shaded areas over the association that couples share. Conquering these impediments requires boldness, understanding, and an undaunted obligation to one another's satisfaction and prosperity.

Distinguishing and Tending to Obstructions

The most vital phase in exploring the difficulties to closeness is the ID of the actual hindrances. Correspondence breakdowns, unsettled clashes, and the stressors of day to day existence can all disintegrate the underpinnings of closeness. Perceiving these issues requests a degree of genuineness and mindfulness from the two accomplices, as well as a readiness to stand up to awkward bits of insight. Tending to these obstructions includes open exchange, where the two people have a real sense of security to communicate their sentiments, fears, and needs. Arrangements might shift from straightforward changes in everyday schedules to looking for outer help, yet the critical lies in the shared obligation to reestablishing the wellbeing and imperativeness of the relationship.

The Job of Pardoning

At the core of defeating numerous hindrances to closeness lies the force of absolution. Held onto complaints and past damages can make walls between companions, hindering the pathways to genuine association. Absolution is the demonstration of destroying these walls, deciding to relinquish hatred and to embrace mending. It is a demonstration of beauty, reflecting the absolution that we most definitely look for and get from God. Through pardoning, couples can find independence from the chains of the past, making the way for a recharged closeness that is based on trust, understanding, and unrestricted love.

Looking for Help When Required

There are times in the excursion of marriage when the hindrances to closeness might demonstrate excessively overwhelming to explore alone. At these times, looking for proficient assistance through guiding or treatment is an indication of solidarity and obligation to the relationship. A talented specialist can offer new points of view, devices, and techniques to help couples comprehend and address the main drivers of their difficulties. This step, frequently removed from a profound love and want to save the obligation of marriage, can be an essential direct in the excursion to mending and more profound closeness.

Conquering snags to closeness isn't an excursion that couples set out on once yet a constant part of the conjugal experience. It requires tolerance, steadiness, and an immovable commitment to one another's bliss. Through this cycle, couples can not just explore the difficulties that come their direction yet in addition arise more grounded, more associated, and more profoundly enamored than any time in recent memory. It is through confronting and beating these difficulties together that the genuine strength and profundity of a conjugal security are uncovered, sparkling as a demonstration of the force of adoration, flexibility, and effortlessness.

Supplication and Closeness

In the hallowed pledge of marriage, petitioning heaven remains as a strong course for closeness, winding around together the profound strings that tight spot hearts in an association that reflects the heavenly. Supplication, when divided among life partners, turns out to be considerably more than a ceremonial expression; it changes into a significant articulation of adoration, weakness, and shared dependence on God's direction and insight.

Developing Closeness Through Petition

Shared petitioning God welcomes couples into a space of unrivaled closeness, where the most profound cravings of their souls are uncovered before one another and their Maker. At these times, couples speak with God as well as with each other, on a level that rises above words. This otherworldly closeness encourages a one of a kind bond, as the two people adjust their expectations, fears, and dreams with God's will, drawing strength from their unified confidence.

The demonstration of imploring together empowers a degree of weakness and trust that is fundamental for the development of closeness. It permits every life partner to see the other's heart, to grasp their battles and yearnings, and to remain in fortitude with them in their profound excursion. This common weakness turns into the bedrock of a profound and persevering through association, one that is continually fed by the beauty and love of God.

Petition as a Wellspring of Solace and Strength

Life, with its inescapable difficulties and preliminaries, can test the obligations of marriage. During circumstances such as the present, petitioning heaven arises as a wellspring of solace and strength, an encouraging sign that enlightens the way ahead. At the point when couples go to petition in snapshots of trouble, they are helped to remember the presence of God, who is with them in each preliminary. This information brings a feeling of harmony and confirmation, supporting the solidarity among them and engaging them to confront difficulties along with confidence and mental fortitude.

Supplication brings solace as well as sustains the relationship, giving a profound defensive layer that secures and reinforces the conjugal bond. It is in looking for God's insight and resting on His solidarity that couples track down the flexibility to explore life's tempests, arising sound as well as reinforced by their preliminaries.

Developing a Propensity for Supplication

For supplication to completely show its power in a marriage, it should be developed as a reliable propensity, woven into the texture of day to day existence. This requires purposefulness and responsibility, as couples go with the decision to focus on petition in the midst of the requests of their timetables. Laying out normal times for petition, whether in the calm of the morning, the tranquility of the evening, or suddenly over the course of the day, guarantees that correspondence with God stays at the core of the relationship.

Couples can investigate different types of supplication, from intercessory petitions and thanksgiving to insightful and reflective supplications, finding together the practices that attract them nearer to God and to one another. The key is diligence and receptiveness to the main of the Essence of God, permitting supplication to advance and develop over the long run.

In the excursion of marriage, petitioning heaven isn't only an otherworldly discipline yet a significant articulation of adoration and a crucial device for building closeness. Through supplication, couples can explore the intricacies of existence with beauty, move nearer to God, and produce a bond that is established in the timeless. It is in the sacrosanct space of shared supplication that the genuine substance of a Divine being focused marriage is uncovered, blooming into a relationship that mirrors the excellence, strength, and profundity of heavenly love.

Chapter 6: Financial Stewardship in a Christian Marriage

Laying out a Scriptural Viewpoint on Cash

In the core of a Christian marriage, several perspectives and deals with their funds can be an impression of their confidence and confidence in God's arrangement. Laying out a scriptural point of view on cash is primary to exploring the monetary parts of marriage such that respects God and reinforces the conjugal bond.

Grasping Cash from a Scriptural Perspective

The Holy book offers significant insight on the subject of riches and assets, introducing an unmistakably alternate point of view from the perspective. Sacred texts instruct that all that we have is a gift from God and that we are stewards of His assets (Hymn 24:1). This stewardship is an obligation that calls for savvy the board, liberality, and a dependence on God as opposed to on material riches. By understanding cash from a scriptural perspective, couples can approach their monetary choices inside the setting of their confidence, perceiving that their actual security and worth are found in God, not in their ledgers.

Embracing this viewpoint includes a change in outlook where cash is seen not as an end in itself but rather as a device for achieving God's motivations. It challenges the social story of commercialization and independence, empowering couples to rely upon God's arrangement and to involve their assets in manners that mirror His affection and liberality.

Adjusting Monetary Objectives to Profound Qualities

For Christian couples, adjusting monetary objectives to profound qualities is a basic move toward guaranteeing that their funds fill a more noteworthy need than simple individual solace or security. This arrangement starts with determined thought of what values are most significant in their coexistence — like liberality, accommodation, or preacher support — and how these qualities can be communicated through their monetary preparation.

Couples are urged to define monetary objectives that meet their reasonable requirements as well as empower them to add to their congregation, support missions, and help those out of luck. This could mean focusing on investment funds for individual future requirements as well as for potential chances to give and serve. It could likewise include pursuing way of life decisions that let loose assets for more noteworthy liberality, like living underneath their means or embracing a less complex way of life.

Laying out a scriptural viewpoint on cash and adjusting monetary objectives to otherworldly qualities are demonstrations of trust that can profoundly improve a marriage. They require trust in God's arrangement, open correspondence, and common settlement on monetary needs. By establishing their monetary choices in their confidence, couples can make a monetary arrangement that gets their future as well as mirrors their obligation to experiencing their Christian qualities. This way to deal with funds turns into a day to day articulation of their confidence in God and their craving to involve His gifts for His greatness, reinforcing their marriage and their confidence simultaneously.

Making and Dealing with a Joint Spending plan

The foundation of a brought together monetary arrangement, especially a joint spending plan, remains as a demonstration of the responsibility and organization inborn in a Christian marriage. It is a step of faith, straightforwardness, and common objectives, intelligent of the couple's devotion to managing God's gifts astutely and supporting each other in their common life venture.

The Significance of a Brought together Monetary Arrangement

A joint spending plan is something other than a bookkeeping sheet specifying pay and costs; it is an unmistakable articulation of a couple's common dreams, needs, and values. With regards to Christian steward-ship, making a bound together monetary arrangement is an affirmation that all assets are given by God and ought to be utilized in a way that praises Him. This approach encourages a feeling of solidarity, as the two accomplices effectively participate in choices that influence their present and future, guaranteeing that their monetary practices mirror their obligation to one another and to experiencing their confidence.

The demonstration of planning together empowers open corre-spondence about funds, a subject that can frequently be a wellspring of pressure in relationships. Through normal spending plan gatherings, couples have the chance to talk about their monetary circumstance transparently, set present moment and long haul objectives, and address any worries or changes required. This continuous exchange assembles trust and guarantees that the two people are adjusted in their monetary excursion, cooperating towards normal goals.

Commonsense Strides for Planning Together

The most common way of making and dealing with a joint financial plan starts with a thorough survey of the couple's pay, costs, obligations, and reserve funds. This outline gives a reasonable image of their mone-tary wellbeing and fills in as an establishment for laying out sensible and reachable objectives. Couples are urged to sort their costs into neces-sities, needs, and reserve funds/giving, focusing on their spending in a way that mirrors their Christian qualities and monetary objectives.

Then, saving assets for giving and beneficent giving toward the start of the planning system supports the standard of liberality as funda-mentally important, not a reconsideration. This training epitomizes the scriptural educating of giving the principal natural products to

God, recognizing His arrangement and communicating trust in His proceeded with care.

Compelling financial plan the board likewise includes normal checking and changing of the financial plan as needs be. Life conditions change, and a spending plan that once served the couple well might require modifications to oblige new objectives or surprising costs. These changes ought to be made together, with the two accomplices adding to the dynamic interaction.

Making and dealing with a joint spending plan is a dynamic and progressing process that requires persistence, discipline, and an eagerness to learn and become together. It is a priceless device for building monetary solidarity and responsibility inside a marriage, giving a structure to couples to reliably steward their assets such that praises God and reinforces their relationship. Through this cooperative exertion, couples can accomplish monetary security, seek after their common objectives, and experience the delight and opportunity of living inside God's arrangement.

Handling Obligation and Anticipating What's to come

In the stewardship of their funds, Christian couples face the double test of overseeing present commitments while getting ready for future requirements. A reasonable way to deal with handling obligation and making arrangements for what's in store isn't just judicious yet in addition well established in scriptural standards of shrewdness and prescience.

Procedures for Obligation Decrease

The excursion towards independence from the rat race frequently starts with a guarantee to paying off past commitments. Precepts 22:7 cautions, "The rich rule over poor people, and the borrower is slave to the loan specialist." Perceiving the servitude that obligation makes, it becomes basic for couples to devise and execute a brilliant course of action for its end. This cycle begins with a legit evaluation, everything being equal, trailed by the prioritization of reimbursement in view of loan costs, balances, and the potential for diminishing in general interest paid.

One compelling procedure is the obligation snowball strategy, which includes taking care of obligations from littlest to biggest, paying little mind to loan cost, to gather speed and inspiration. On the other hand, the obligation torrential slide technique centers around squaring away obligations with the most noteworthy loan costs first, possibly setting aside more cash over the long run. No matter what the technique picked, the key is consistency, responsibility, and correspondence, guaranteeing the two accomplices are adjusted and steady of the procedure.

Long haul Monetary Preparation

While tending to current obligations, couples should likewise project their look forward, making arrangements for future monetary necessities. This incorporates putting something aside for crises, contributing for retirement, and taking into account protection needs. Laying out a backup stash is a basic initial step, giving a monetary support that can forestall the gathering of new obligation even with unforeseen costs.

For retirement arranging, couples are urged to make the most of manager supported retirement plans, individual retirement accounts (IRAs), and other venture open doors. The rule of accumulated dividends highlights the insight of beginning these reserve funds early, permitting time to develop the speculation. In the mean time, life and medical coverage assume pivotal parts in shielding against unexpected medical problems or occasions, safeguarding the family's monetary security.

Trust in God's Arrangement

In the meantime, couples actually should keep up with their confidence in God's arrangement. Philippians 4:19 guarantees, "And my God will address every one of your issues as per the wealth of his greatness in Christ Jesus." Offsetting savvy monetary stewardship with confidence in God's timing and arrangement dodges the traps of uneasiness and debilitation. Normal petition for direction, astuteness, and acumen in monetary choices welcomes God into the stewardship cycle, adjusting monetary practices to divine needs.

In handling obligation and making arrangements for the future, Christian couples participate in an unmistakable articulation of their confidence and stewardship. This excursion, set apart by discipline, shared objectives, and confidence in God, prompts independence from the rat race as well as reinforces the conjugal bond, establishing a strong starting point for a future that praises God and serves His realm.

The Job of Liberality and Giving

In the core of a Christian marriage, liberality remains as a reference point of the couple's obligation to mirroring God's affection and arrangement. The demonstration of giving, both giving to the congregation and adding to worthy missions, is an honest strong articulation, trust, and compliance to God's Promise. From this perspective of liberality couples can really encounter the delight and satisfaction that comes from carrying on with a daily existence in support of God and others.

Embracing a Way of life of Liberality

Sacred writing is packed with reprimands to live liberally, a way of life that reflects the personality of God Himself, who gave His main Child for our salvation (John 3:16). For Christian couples, embracing a way of life of liberality implies perceiving all that they have as gifts from God, to be utilized for their own advantage, however for the greatness of God and the benefit of His realm. This attitude moves the concentration from aggregation for individual increase to stewardship for everlasting effect.

Liberality isn't restricted by the size of one's abundance yet is portrayed by the ability to give uninhibitedly and cheerfully, as per what one has been given by God (2 Corinthians 9:7). Couples are urged to ask together for wisdom about where and how to offer, looking for open doors that line up with God's heart for poor people, the abused, and the spread of the Gospel.

Viable Ways Of giving as a Couple

Integrating surrendering to their monetary arrangement, couples can begin by focusing on a standard offering to their nearby church, a scriptural rule that respects God as the supplier of all things and supports crafted by the congregation locally and then some. Past giving, couples can recognize magnanimous associations, missions, or causes that resound with their common qualities and interests, saving a piece of their pay to help these undertakings.

Liberality can likewise stretch out past monetary commitments, including the giving of time, gifts, and assets. Chipping in together at a neighborhood cover, taking part in mission excursions, or offering cordiality in their house are only a couple of ways couples can carry on with out a liberal way of life that favors others and commends God.

The Effect of Liberality on Marriage

The demonstration of providing together cultivates a more profound solidarity and motivation in marriage, moving couples nearer as they witness the effect of their liberality on the existences of others. It develops appreciation, lowliness, and a more noteworthy reliance on God, testing the social standards of commercialization and narcissism. Besides, encountering the delight and gift that comes from giving can strengthen a couple's confidence, giving striking tokens of God's steadfastness and the force of His adoration managing them.

Liberality, when polished as a primary standard of monetary stewardship in marriage, improves the relationship in significant ways. It opens the hearts of couples to God's extraordinary work, in their funds as well as in each part of their lives, setting a strong model for people in the future and demonstrating the veracity of the limitless liberality of God Himself. Through the discipline of giving, Christian couples can genuinely encounter the opportunity and satisfaction that come from holding their assets with open hands, fit to be utilized for the greatness of God's realm.

Chapter 7: Parenting and Family Life

Laying out a Christ-focused Home

In the excursion of Christian being a parent, the production of a Christ-focused home stands as both a central objective and an everyday practice. It is inside the walls of the home that kids initially find out about God's adoration, the bits of insight Who can certainly be trusted, and the excellence of carrying on with a daily existence dedicated to Christ. Laying out such a home requires purposeful exertion, attached in the craving to mesh confidence into the actual texture of day to day life, establishing a climate where each collaboration mirrors the beauty, love, and reality of the gospel.

Underpinnings of a Confidence filled Family

A confidence filled family is based upon the strong stone of Christ's lessons, where His Statement guides choices, connections, and the general ethos of the family. This establishment is laid by routinely captivating with the Good book as a family, through commitments, supplication, and open conversations about sacred text. It includes making schedules that focus on profound disciplines, implanting them into the everyday mood of day to day life. Guardians can cultivate a rich, confidence filled climate by integrating love music, Christian writing, and scriptural narrating into their kids' lives, making the information on God open and drawing in since early on.

Down to earth articulations of confidence are additionally fundamental. This could incorporate gift dinners, offering supplications of thanksgiving and request in both cheerful and testing times, and perceiving God's craftsmanship in the excellence of daily existence. Such practices help to develop a feeling of God's presence and action in and around the family, supporting reality that confidence isn't bound to Sunday benefits however is a lively, living reality consistently.

Job Demonstrating and Profound Administration

Guardians are the essential otherworldly pioneers and good examples for their youngsters, typifying the standards of the Christian confidence in their activities, choices, and connections. This authority isn't about flawlessness yet legitimacy, showing a certifiable quest for Christ and an eagerness to depend on His effortlessness in snapshots of disappointment or shortcoming. By straightforwardly sharing their confidence process, including battles and triumphs, guardians can offer their youngsters a practical image of what a no nonsense confidence seems to be.

Otherworldly administration includes directing youngsters in petition, helping them to look for God's insight, to tune in for His voice, and to answer His call. It additionally implies displaying Christ-like love and administration, showing kids the significance of really focusing on others, broadening absolution, and looking for compromise. This initiative isn't practiced through power yet through subjugation and love, mirroring Jesus' own way to deal with authority inside His apprenticeship.

Laying out a Christ-focused home is a mission loaded up with difficulties and wins. It requires tirelessness, supplication, and a consistent dependence on God's solidarity and intelligence. Be that as it may, the prizes are everlasting, as guardians have the real, significant honor of driving their kids into a caring relationship with their Maker, making way for a long period and commitment. In doing as such, they improve their family's otherworldly life as well as add to the fortifying of their congregation local area and the more extensive Realm of God.

Exploring Nurturing Difficulties with Elegance

Nurturing, in its pith, is an excursion set apart by both gigantic happiness and huge difficulties. A calling requires thinking, tolerance, and a wealth of elegance. Christian guardians are entrusted with directing their youngsters through the coordinated factors of life as well as through the intricacies of filling in confidence and character. In that capacity, exploring nurturing difficulties with beauty turns into a significant part of making a supporting, Christ-focused home climate.

Tending to Teach and Direction

Discipline and direction are vital parts of nurturing, established in affection and pointed toward sustaining the youngster's heart towards Faithful insight and nobility. The scriptural way to deal with discipline includes something beyond adjustment; it's tied in with directing kids towards understanding their activities, the results thereof, and the better decisions accessible to them. Ephesians 6:4 teaches guardians to "bring them up in the discipline and guidance of the Ruler." This implies discipline ought to be controlled in a manner that mirrors God's own personality — reliable, just, and consistently roused by adoration.

Successful direction requires correspondence that is open, genuine, and humane, permitting youngsters to communicate their sentiments and contemplations unafraid of judgment. This cultivates a climate of trust where examples can be gained from discipline as well as through the results of one's activities, directed by parental insight and scriptural bits of insight. Guardians are urged to appeal to God for astuteness in dealing with disciplinary issues, looking for God's direction in every circumstance to know when to offer firm direction and when to broaden elegance.

Overseeing Relational intricacies

Everyday life is innately powerful, portrayed by various characters, phases of development, and individual requirements. Dealing with these elements in a manner that advances harmony, solidarity, and otherworldly development requires a beauty filled approach. It begins with perceiving the singularity of every relative, appreciating their interesting commitments to the family, and grasping their own difficulties and necessities.

Struggle is an inescapable part of relational intricacies, yet it additionally presents open doors for showing significant qualities like pardoning, compromise, and the force of effortlessness. Guardians assume a significant part in intervening struggles, showing how to determine conflicts in a way that respects God and fortifies connections. This could include showing kids how to impart really, how to listen compassionately, and how to apologize and excuse earnestly.

Empowering open exchange about confidence, life's inquiries, and individual battles can likewise reinforce family bonds and cultivate a climate where each part feels esteemed and heard. Such a climate not just aides in exploring the ordinary difficulties of day to day life yet in addition in confronting outside tensions and impacts with solidarity and flexibility.

Exploring nurturing difficulties with elegance isn't a call flawlessly yet to tirelessness and dedication. It's tied in with resting on God's solidarity and shrewdness, constantly looking for His direction through supplication, and confiding in His sovereign arrangement for every relative. By tending to train with adoration and overseeing relational peculiarities with understanding and effortlessness, guardians can direct their youngsters through the intricacies of life while sustaining their development in confidence and character.

Encouraging Family Solidarity and Love

In the complicated dance of everyday life, encouraging solidarity and love is likened to developing a nursery; it calls for investment, persistence, and the day to day supporting of connections to completely blossom. A Christian home blossoms with the standards of adoration, regard, and shared help, mirroring the solidarity and caring affection tracked down in the connection among Christ and the Congregation. This part digs into pragmatic procedures for building solid family bonds and establishing a supporting climate where every part can develop separately and together in confidence.

Building Solid Bonds Through Quality Time

Quality time is the foundation of family solidarity. It's the purposeful, full focus guardians provide for their kids, making minutes that form enduring recollections and extend connections. These minutes don't necessarily should be amazing or carefully arranged; they can be basically as straightforward as sharing dinners without the interruption of innovation, evening strolls, or sleep time stories. What is important is the presence, the present time and place, completely captivating with one another in significant exercises that encourage a feeling of having a place and love.

Laying out family customs and ceremonies likewise assumes a critical part in serious areas of strength for building. These can be week by week occasions like family game evenings, or yearly customs, for example, special festivals or summer setting up camp excursions. Such practices give a feeling of progression, personality, and having a place that re-inforces the nuclear family, making an embroidery of shared encounters that structure the background of your family's exceptional story.

Empowering Individual and Aggregate Development

While encouraging solidarity is fundamental, supporting the singular development of every relative is similarly significant. Perceiving and praising every individual's exceptional abilities, interests, and profound gifts supports a culture of common regard and appreciation. Guardians can develop this by giving open doors to individual articulation and improvement, whether through sports, expressions, scholarly pursuits, or otherworldly disciplines like petition and Book of scriptures study.

Aggregate development as a family is sustained through shared objectives and values, which could incorporate help projects, mission trips, or taking part in chapel exercises together. These common encounters not just add to the family's profound and close to home development yet additionally build up the upsides of sympathy, administration, and confidence in real life.

Cultivating family solidarity and love is a unique cycle that adjusts as the family develops and changes over the long haul. It's tied in with tracking down balance — celebrating individual accomplishments while supporting a feeling of aggregate personality and reason. By focusing on quality connections, laying out significant practices, and empowering both individual and aggregate development, families can make a cherishing, steady climate where each part feels esteemed, comprehended, and associated.

This supporting environment turns into the dirt from which confidence can thrive, implanting a tradition of affection and solidarity that rises above ages. It's in this rich ground that kids become familiar with the genuine quintessence of Christian living — through the lessons of Sacred text as well as through the lived illustration of affection and solidarity in their own loved ones.

Drawing in with the More extensive Local area and Church

The Christian family, while a real safe-haven and love, isn't intended to be a separate unit. It flourishes and enhances its confidence through dynamic commitment with the more extensive local area and the collection of Christ. This outward center not just embodies the call to be salt and light on the planet yet in addition shows relatives, particularly youngsters, the worth of administration, local area, and the different ways God deals with His kin.

The Family's Job in the Congregation and Local area

The early church in Acts showed a strong model of collective residing, where devotees shared their lives, assets, and confidence with each other. In this advanced period, Christian families are called to typify this soul of local area by effectively partaking in their neighborhood places of worship and stretching out their support of the more extensive local area. This can include serving in chapel services, joining or driving little gatherings, and partaking in local area outreach programs. Participating in these exercises not just reinforces the family's association with their confidence local area yet in addition gives a stage to rehearsing servanthood, neighborliness, and evangelism.

Contribution in chapel and local area shows kids the significance of partnership and administration since early on, imbuing in them a feeling of obligation and delight in adding to the government assistance of others. It likewise opens them to different points of view and needs, widening how they might interpret the world and developing sympathy and a worker hearted mentality.

Showing Social Obligation and Administration

A critical part of drawing in with the more extensive local area is showing kids the standards of social obligation and administration. This includes assisting them with grasping the requirements of others, both locally and worldwide, and empowering them to consider ways they can have an effect. Guardians can show others how its done, including the entire family in help projects, mission outings, or nearby chipping in open doors. These encounters encourage a heart for administration as well as give commonsense lifestyle choices out the Gospel.

In addition, families can rehearse friendliness by opening their homes to neighbors, church individuals, or those out of luck, epitomizing the adoration and welcome of Christ. This training builds up the message that Christianity isn't just about going to community gatherings yet about experiencing one's confidence in substantial, significant ways.

Building a Tradition of Confidence and Administration

Drawing in with the more extensive local area and church isn't just about the quick effect; it's tied in with building a tradition of confidence and administration. At the point when kids see their folks experiencing their confidence through help, friendliness, and local area contribution, they learn priceless illustrations about affection, penance, and the groundbreaking force of the Gospel. These illustrations become imbued in their souls, molding their perspective and directing their own excursion of confidence and administration.

All in all, a Christian family's commitment with the more extensive local area and church is an essential part of their aggregate profound excursion. It fortifies the family's confidence, shows significant illustrations of administration and obligation, and effects the world with the affection for Christ. By venturing past the solace of their home and into the more extensive local area, families can encounter the significant bliss and satisfaction that comes from serving together, building a tradition of confidence that reverberations through ages.

Chapter 8: Overcoming Challenges Together

Perceiving and Tending to Outside Tensions

In the excursion of marriage, couples frequently end up exploring a scene set apart by different outside pressures. These tensions, whether monetary challenges, business related pressure, social assumptions, or the requests of nurturing, can essentially influence the wellbeing and bliss of a marriage. Perceiving and successfully tending to these outside pressures are essential moves toward protecting the conjugal bond and keeping a Christ-focused relationship.

Recognizing Outside Stressors

The most important phase in conquering outer tensions is to plainly distinguish them. This includes legitimate and open correspondence between life partners about the difficulties every individual is confronting, whether in the work environment, inside the more distant family, or from cultural assumptions. Monetary troubles, quite possibly of the most widely recognized stressor, can strain a marriage when not tended to straightforwardly and with a unified front. Business related pressure, as well, can pour out over into the home, influencing a couple's connection and quality time together. Social assumptions, for example, the strain to keep a specific way of life or to parent with a certain goal in mind, can likewise make excessive pressure.

Recognizing these tensions together permits couples to move from confronting them as people to handling them collectively. This common acknowledgment is the most important move toward fostering an essential methodology grounded in confidence and shared help.

Techniques for Moderating Outside Tensions

When outside pressures have been distinguished, couples can utilize a few procedures to relieve their effect. A foundation of this approach is the dependence on God's solidarity and shrewdness, welcoming Him into the circumstance through supplication and looking for His direction in Sacred writing. Philippians 4:6-7 urges devotees not to be restless about everything except rather in each circumstance, by supplication and appeal, with thanksgiving, to introduce their solicitations to God. This heavenly harmony can monitor hearts and psyches, offering comfort and strength in the midst of outer difficulties.

Viable correspondence is another basic technique. By consistently talking about their interests, fears, and dissatisfactions, couples can uphold each other sincerely and cooperate to track down functional arrangements. Defining limits around work hours, restricting monetary responsibilities, or diminishing social commitment can assist with decreasing the tension on the conjugal relationship.

Also, defining boundaries as per God's will can assist couples with knowing which tensions require their consideration and which can be delivered. This could mean improving on their lives to zero in additional on the main thing, for example, their relationship with God and one another, as opposed to endeavoring to measure up to each outside assumption.

In confronting outer tensions, couples are reminded that their solidarity comes from their solidarity in Christ. By resting on God, conveying straightforwardly, and defining limits, they can explore the difficulties of coexistence, protecting and reinforcing their marriage even with any outside stressor. This excursion, however full of difficulties, is likewise a chance for development, attracting couples nearer to one another and to God as they defeat the tensions of the world together.

Exploring Struggles under the surface

While outside tensions can strain a marriage, unseen struggles frequently represent a more straightforward test to the concordance and flexibility of the conjugal bond. These contentions, emerging from neglected assumptions, correspondence breakdowns, or varying qualities and convictions, request cautious route. Resolving these issues with elegance, understanding, and a guarantee to development is indispensable for couples endeavoring to keep areas of strength for a, focused relationship.

Grasping the Underlying foundations of Contention

The beginning of struggle under the surface in a marriage frequently lies in neglected assumptions. These can come from assumptions about conjugal jobs, obligations, or how love and friendship ought to be communicated. At the point when reality doesn't line up with these assumptions, disillusionment and contact can result. Correspondence breakdowns further fuel these issues, prompting false impressions and hatred. Moreover, contrasts in values, convictions, or needs can make breaks in the event that not tended to with sympathy and transparency.

Perceiving the fundamental reasons for struggle is the most important move towards goal. This requires legitimate self-reflection and an eagerness to pay attention to one's accomplice without preventiveness. James 1:19 exhorts, "Everybody ought to rush to tune in, slow to talk and ease back to end up being irate," a rule that holds significant insight for overseeing conjugal questions. By trying to comprehend prior to being perceived, couples can connect holes and figure out some mutual interest.

Helpful Compromise

Helpful compromise in marriage isn't around one accomplice winning and the other losing however about finding arrangements that fortify the relationship. This cycle starts with open, conscious correspondence, where the two accomplices have a good sense of security to communicate their sentiments and viewpoints. It's vital to talk reality in affection, resolving issues straightforwardly while staying away from fault or analysis that can prompt additionally stung.

Petitioning heaven assumes a urgent part in exploring unseen struggles. By imploring together for shrewdness, persistence, and understanding, couples welcome God to work in their souls and their relationship, changing difficulties into amazing open doors for development and extending closeness.

Pardoning is one more basic component of valuable compromise. Ephesians 4:32 calls devotees to "be caring and humane to each other, excusing one another, similarly as in Christ God pardoned you." Clutching outrage or disdain can harm a marriage from the back to front. Absolution, then again, discharges that toxic substance, permitting recuperating and compromise to occur.

At long last, looking for shared belief and compromising where conceivable exhibits a promise to the strength of the marriage over individual inclinations. This might require adaptability, inventiveness, and once in a while proficient guiding to explore complex issues. Nonetheless, the work to determine clashes productively is a demonstration of the couple's commitment to their pledge with one another and with God.

Exploring unseen struggles with elegance, shrewdness, and a guarantee to solidarity is fundamental for keeping areas of strength for a, marriage. Through fair correspondence, supplication, pardoning, and an eagerness to think twice about, can defeat interior difficulties, developing nearer to one another and to God simultaneously.

Reinforcing the Conjugal Bond in Preliminaries

Misfortune is a certain piece of life, and several faces preliminaries can significantly mean for the strength and profundity of their conjugal security. These times of difficulty — whether they come from medical problems, misfortune, or outside emergencies — test the versatility of a relationship. However, it is inside these very preliminaries that the chance for critical development and extending of the conjugal bond lies. By inclining toward their confidence in God and one another, couples can rise out of these seasons flawless as well as braced.

The Job of Confidence in Beating Difficulty

Vital to exploring preliminaries together is a common confidence in God. This confidence gives a solid groundwork when the tempests of life take steps to overpower. It is the affirmation of things expected, the conviction of things not seen (Jews 11:1). In snapshots of depression or vulnerability, going to supplication and Sacred text offers couples strength and point of view, advising them that they are in good company in their battles. God is with them, a resolute presence offering solace, direction, and trust.

Confidence in God's power and goodness permits couples to see their preliminaries from a perspective of trust. Believe that, regardless of the result, God is working for their great and the development of their confidence (Romans 8:28). This point of view urges couples to rest on God and one another, cultivating a profound feeling of solidarity and reason as they face difficulties together.

Down to earth Ways to keep up with Solidarity and Love

Keeping up with solidarity and love during preliminaries requires deliberate exertion. It includes open correspondence about fears, dissatisfactions, and requirements, guaranteeing that the two accomplices feel appreciated and upheld. Consistently making opportunity to interface, whether through supplication, discussion, or essentially being together, can assist with keeping up with close to home closeness and common comprehension.

Shared petitioning God is especially strong during testing times. Preceding God as a team, lifting up their interests, and looking for His insight and harmony attracts them nearer to Him and one another. A holy season of weakness and trust can reinforce the conjugal bond in significant ways.

Demonstrations of administration and confirmation are likewise urgent. Little tokens of affection and appreciation can be unquestionably significant when one or the two accomplices are battling. Whether it's taking on additional obligations around the house, offering uplifting statements, or basically holding space for one another's agony, these thoughtful gestures show love in real life.

In conclusion, reaffirming obligation to one another is imperative. Helping each other to remember the promises to remain by each other "in disorder and in wellbeing, for more extravagant or less fortunate" can be a strong wellspring of solace and strength. It highlights the pledge made before God, restricting the couple along with a responsibility that rises above the preliminaries they face.

Preliminaries can possibly either split apart couples or unite them. By establishing their relationship in confidence, embracing open correspondence, taking part in shared petition, and showing demonstrations of affection and responsibility, couples can explore these difficulties with effortlessness. Such a methodology doesn't simply assist them with persevering; it permits them to develop together, extending their confidence in God and one another, and eventually fortifying their conjugal bond in manners that no one but misfortune can.

Looking for Help and Direction

The excursion of marriage, particularly in the midst of challenge, isn't intended to be explored in disengagement. Looking for help and direction is a demonstration of the strength of a couple's obligation to sustaining and saving their relationship. It recognizes the intricacy of human connections and the insight tracked down in the collection of Christ — the congregation, confided in companions, and experts. This outer help can give significant viewpoint, support, and reasonable exhortation, assisting couples with conquering impediments and develop nearer through their preliminaries.

The Significance of Local area and Guiding

The Christian people group, including the neighborhood church and little gatherings, fills in as an essential wellspring of help for wedded couples. Inside this local area, couples track down not just profound food through shared confidence and petition yet in addition functional exhortation and consistent encouragement from the people who have confronted comparative difficulties. The congregation body can reflect God's adoration and care, offering an update that two or three needs to confront their preliminaries alone.

For certain difficulties, particularly those that are well established or complex, looking for proficient guiding can be a priceless step. Christian instructors or specialists can offer direction that lines up with scriptural standards, giving a place of refuge to couples to investigate the underlying foundations of their struggles, recuperate from past injuries, and foster better examples of correspondence and cooperation. This expert help supplements profound direction, tending to the mental and close to home parts of the relationship with skill and compassion.

Utilizing Otherworldly Assets

Notwithstanding people group backing and expert guiding, couples are urged to use otherworldly assets. Supplication, both individual and shared, is an incredible asset for looking for God's direction and strength. It welcomes help from above into the difficulties being confronted, encouraging a more profound dependence on God's insight and timing.

Drawing in with Sacred text offers one more layer of help, giving immortal insight, solace, and support. The Holy book is loaded with accounts of people and couples who confronted gigantic preliminaries yet arose fortified by their confidence. These accounts can offer expectation and viewpoint, helping couples to remember God's dedication and His vows to accompany them in each situation.

Profound mentorship from additional accomplished Christian couples can likewise give direction and consolation. These guides can share bits of knowledge from their own excursions, offering functional exhortation and profound insight that can assist with exploring the intricacies of marriage.

Looking for help and direction even with conjugal difficulties is a demonstration of boldness and modesty. It recognizes the restrictions of human insight and the force of local area, guiding, and otherworldly assets in giving strength, astuteness, and mending. By connecting for help, couples exhibit their obligation to one another and their dependence on God, situating their marriage for development, recuperating, and more profound solidarity. Along these lines, the preliminaries confronted can become impetuses for change, advancing the conjugal relationship and extending the couple's confidence.

Conclusion: Continuing the Journey Together

Embracing Long lasting Learning

Marriage, in its embodiment, is an excursion of nonstop development and revelation. As couples explore the consistently changing scenes of coexistence, the obligation to deep rooted learning turns into a foundation of a solid, dynamic relationship. This responsibility isn't just about getting new information or abilities yet about developing getting it, sympathy, and love for each other under the direction of God's everlasting insight.

Obligation to Development

At the core of embracing deep rooted learning is the acknowledgment that the two people and their relationship will develop over the long haul. Change is an inescapable piece of life and marriage. Couples who focus on becoming together, instead of opposing or dreading change, are better prepared to confront the future certainly and unitedly. This development includes otherworldly and profound aspects as well as scholarly, physical, and social perspectives. It includes effectively looking for open doors for advancement, whether through perusing, going to studios or meetings, taking part in significant discussions, or basically being available to new encounters together.

A guarantee to development likewise implies being proactive in resolving issues and difficulties as they emerge, as opposed to allowing them to putrefy or heighten. It includes consistently assessing the well-being of the relationship, speaking the truth about regions that need consideration, and enthusiastically looking for help or guidance when fundamental. This proactive position assists with guaranteeing that the marriage makes due as well as flourishes, mirroring the dynamic, living nature of God's creation.

Receptiveness to Change

Embracing long lasting advancing additionally requires a receptiveness to change. Life brings different seasons, each with its own arrangement of difficulties and delights. From the fervor and changes of love bird life to the intricacies of raising a family, profession changes, and in the long run maturing, each period of life influences the conjugal relationship in special ways. Being available to change implies seeing these advances as any open doors for development and extending closeness, as opposed to dangers to the norm.

This transparency reaches out to each accomplice's self-improvement and change. Throughout the long term, people might find new interests, foster alternate points of view, or go through critical otherworldly encounters. Inviting and supporting each other's development encourages a dynamic and improving relationship, grounded in shared regard and love.

All in all, embracing long lasting advancing inside marriage is about something other than confronting change together; it's about effectively chasing after development, directed by God's insight and effortlessness. About sustaining a relationship mirrors the consistently inventive, steadily cherishing nature of God Himself. As couples focus on this excursion of deep rooted learning, they fabricate an enduring marriage as well as a signal of God's groundbreaking adoration on the planet.

Developing Day to day Propensities for Adoration and Confidence

In the texture of a solid, getting through marriage, the strings are the day to day propensities for affection and confidence that couples wind around together. These practices structure the daily schedule of association that supports the relationship, guaranteeing that, notwithstanding the inescapable back and forth movement of life's requests, the underpinning of the marriage stays strong and versatile. Developing these propensities is a continuous interaction, one that requires deliberateness, devotion, and the beauty of God to prosper.

Building an Everyday practice of Association

The daily practice of association between companions isn't about fabulous signals or rare demonstrations of sentiment; rather, it's found in the basic, regular minutes that connote love and responsibility. Imploring together every morning, sharing contemplations and reflections over some espresso, focusing on continuous discussions, and guaranteeing that every day finishes with articulations of appreciation and love are rehearses that reinforce the connection between accomplices.

These propensities act as tokens of the couple's obligation to one another and to God, giving a steady musicality amidst life's confusion. They make a space for weakness, where fears, expectations, dreams, and dissatisfactions can be shared transparently and gotten with effortlessness. In this hallowed space, the conjugal bond develops, in profound closeness as well as in otherworldly solidarity, as couples move nearer to God and to one another.

Building up the Establishment

Key to these everyday propensities is the work to reinforce the marriage's otherworldly establishment. This includes drawing in with Sacred text, separately as well as a team, permitting God's Statement to offer them some sound advice, guide their choices, and shape their relationship. It's tied in with focusing on contribution in chapel and little gathering exercises, where the help and cooperation of the more extensive Christian people group can be a wellspring of consolation, responsibility, and development.

Developing a daily schedule of otherworldly trains likewise implies committing time for joint reflection and petition, bringing before God the delights and difficulties of the marriage. At these times, couples recognize their reliance on God's beauty, look for His insight, and observe His devotion. This otherworldly mooring not just enhances the individual and aggregate confidence venture yet additionally supports the flexibility of the marriage against outside pressures and struggles under the surface.

All in all, the development of day to day propensities for affection and confidence isn't a recipe for an issue free marriage however a procedure for building a relationship that can endure the everyday hardships and situation. By purposefully meshing these practices into the texture of their lives, couples make a marriage that isn't areas of strength for just versatile yet in addition a living demonstration of the force of God's affection and beauty. Eventually, these day to day propensities are the little, yet significant, demonstrations of unwaveringness that reflect Christ's adoration for the congregation, offering a brief look at the heavenly in the everyday.

Reaffirming the Marriage Contract

Inside the holy excursion of marriage, the demonstration of consistently reaffirming the contract made before God and witnesses remains as a strong demonstration of the persevering through responsibility between companions. This deliberate practice praises the first promises as well as recognizes the development, difficulties, and wins experienced en route. It is an insistence that, notwithstanding the unavoidable changes and times of life, the guarantee to adore, honor, and esteem each other remaining parts steadfast.

Reestablishing Responsibility

The reestablishment of responsibility isn't simply a formal demonstration to be seen on critical commemorations; it is a mentality and a heart act that ought to saturate the everyday existence of a marriage. It includes perceiving that, in each activity and choice, companions have the chance to say "I pick you, once more." This decision is made manifest in the manner in which accomplices pay attention to one another, show appreciation, broaden elegance, and backing each other's fantasies and yearnings. It is apparent in the ability to deal with clashes, to pardon, and to fill together in confidence.

Couples can likewise save times for additional conventional recharges of their commitments, maybe during achievement commemorations or subsequent to exploring especially testing seasons. These minutes act as impactful tokens of their excursion and God's reliability all through. They permit couples to ponder the profundity of their adoration and responsibility, which, similar to a fine wine, can possibly develop more extravagant and more mind boggling after some time.

Observing Achievements

Praising achievements in a marriage is a vital piece of reaffirming the marriage pledge. These festivals are tied in with denoting one more year together as well as about recognizing God's elegance and direction. Every commemoration, each victory over affliction, each time of development adds layers to the conjugal inheritance, improving the embroidered artwork of shared life.

Such festivals give an open door to reflection, appreciation, and restored responsibility. They permit couples to relate the manners by which God has worked in their lives, to share accounts of determination, confidence, and cherish that move and empower others. By purposely denoting these achievements, couples honor their past as well as look forward with trust and expectation to the excursion ahead.

Reaffirming the marriage pledge is a dynamic and consistent cycle that reinforces the groundwork of a Christian marriage. It is a statement that, in a universe of transient expressions of warmth and moving loyalties, the hallowed obligation of marriage stays unflinching. Through everyday decisions, formal promises restoration, and the festival of achievements, couples can extend their solidarity, moving nearer to one another and to God. In doing as such, they take the stand concerning the getting through force of affection, the significance of responsibility, and the unwaveringness of God who supports them through each time of life.

Leaving an Inheritance

The climax of a marriage established in God's affection and directed by His standards is the heritage it leaves, an encouraging sign and loyalty for people in the future and the more extensive local area. This inheritance isn't estimated by material riches or outside accomplishments yet by the affection, trustworthiness, and confidence that portray the relationship. It's a demonstration of the getting through force of a contract made before God, mirroring His perpetual reliability in an impacting world.

Affecting People in the future

The tradition of a Christian marriage stretches out a long ways past the existences of the two individuals in the association. It impacts kids, grandkids, and, surprisingly, those without an immediate genealogy, as the couple's daily routine together fills in as an experiencing illustration of God's plan for marriage. This impact envelops the manner in which accomplices treat each other as well as how they draw in with the world, oversee preliminaries, and encapsulate the adoration for Christ locally.

Kids brought up in a home where love, regard, and confidence are tangible gain proficiency with these qualities naturally. They witness firsthand the force of supplication, the significance of pardoning, and the strength tracked down in solidarity. This essential experience shapes how they might interpret connections, their way to deal with difficulties, and their own confidence process, preparing them to construct their lives on similar standards.

Consolation for the Excursion

To couples at any phase of their marriage, the support to push on in affection and loyalty couldn't possibly be more significant. The excursion of marriage, with its ups and downs, is a significant service, a living message taught through the everyday demonstrations of affection, penance, and responsibility. It's a way set apart by elegance, where slip-ups are valuable open doors for development, and difficulties are stages for God's greatness to be uncovered.

The heritage you leave isn't just about the snapshots of win yet additionally about the flexibility in preliminaries, the picking of happiness in distress, and the constant quest for one another's hearts. It's about the obligation to develop together, moving closer to God with each step, and the steady conviction that, through Him, everything is conceivable.

All things considered, recollect that your marriage is a strong instrument in God's grasp, bound to leave an enduring effect. The affection you share, sustained over a long period, turns into a tradition of confidence, trust, and love that reverberations through the ages, motivating and directing the people who emulate your example. In this way, go ahead, realizing that your process together isn't just about the way you walk yet about the effects you have behind.

Appendices

Resources for Further Study

The journey of building a strong, God-centered marriage is continuous, and further study can enrich and deepen this lifelong commitment. Below are carefully selected resources that offer valuable insights and guidance for couples seeking to explore the themes discussed in this book more deeply.

Books

1. **"The 5 Love Languages: The Secret to Love that Lasts" by Gary Chapman** - Explores the concept of love languages and how understanding your partner's language can transform your relationship.

2. **"Sacred Marriage: What If God Designed Marriage to Make Us Holy More Than to Make Us Happy?" by Gary Thomas** - Offers a perspective that the purpose of marriage is to sanctify, not just to satisfy.

3. **"Love & Respect: The Love She Most Desires; The Respect He Desperately Needs" by Emerson Eggerichs** - Discusses the importance of love and respect in a marriage and how they interplay.

4. **"Boundaries in Marriage" by Henry Cloud and John Townsend** - Guides couples on how to establish healthy boundaries that promote respect and love.

5. **"The Meaning of Marriage: Facing the Complexities of Commitment with the Wisdom of God" by Timothy Keller with Kathy Keller** - Provides a profound, biblical perspective on the purpose of marriage.

Websites

1. **Focus on the Family** - www.focusonthefamily.com A resource-rich site offering marriage advice, practical help, and biblical wisdom.
2. **FamilyLife** - www.familylife.com Provides articles, broadcasts, and resources aimed at helping couples build stronger marriages and families.
3. **The Gottman Institute** - www.gottman.com Offers research-based approaches to strengthening relationships.

Other Resources

- **Marriage Retreats and Workshops**: Many churches and organizations offer retreats and workshops designed to strengthen marriages. These can be great opportunities for couples to spend focused time on their relationship in a supportive environment.

Discussion Questions for Each Chapter
Introduction

1. What motivated you to explore building a God-centered marriage, and how do you hope this book will impact your relationship?
2. Discuss your current practices of faith within your relationship. How do you envision these evolving as you journey through this book?

Chapter 1: Foundations of a Godly Marriage

1. Reflect on the concept of marriage as a covenant with God. How does this perspective influence your understanding and commitment to your marriage?

2. Discuss the roles and responsibilities you each assume in your marriage. How do they reflect your unique strengths and the principles of partnership outlined in Scripture?

Chapter 2: Communication in Marriage

1. Identify areas in your communication that need improvement. How can you apply the principles of effective and loving communication discussed in this chapter?
2. Share a recent instance where miscommunication led to conflict. Discuss how the situation could have been handled differently using strategies from this chapter.

Chapter 3: The Role of Forgiveness and Grace

1. Share a time when forgiveness strengthened your marriage. How did it reflect God's forgiveness?
2. Discuss ways you can cultivate a culture of grace in your marriage, especially during disagreements.

Chapter 4: Growing Together Spiritually

1. What spiritual disciplines do you practice individually and as a couple? How have these practices enriched your relationship?
2. Discuss how you can support each other's spiritual growth. Are there new spiritual practices you would like to explore together?

Chapter 5: Nurturing Intimacy in Marriage

1. How do you define intimacy in your marriage? Discuss ways you can deepen intimacy, both physically and emotionally.
2. Reflect on the role of vulnerability in building intimacy. Share an area where you struggle to be vulnerable and discuss how you can support each other in this.

Chapter 6: Financial Stewardship in a Christian Marriage

1. Discuss your beliefs and practices around financial stewardship. How do they align with the biblical principles outlined in this chapter?
2. Identify one financial goal for your family. Create a plan that reflects stewardship principles to achieve this goal.

Chapter 7: Parenting and Family Life

1. How do you see your parenting styles reflecting your faith? Discuss areas of strength and growth.
2. Share how you can incorporate faith more intentionally into your family life and parenting.

Chapter 8: Overcoming Challenges Together

1. Reflect on a challenge you faced together. How did it impact your marriage, and how did you navigate it?
2. Discuss strategies from this chapter that you can apply to future challenges to strengthen your bond.

Conclusion: Continuing the Journey Together

1. Reflect on the main insights you've gained from this book. How do you plan to implement these in your marriage?
2. Discuss how you envision your legacy as a couple. What steps can you take now to build towards this legacy?

These questions are designed to foster open, heartfelt conversations that will deepen your connection and enhance your journey toward a strong, God-centered marriage.